Chatting with America

by
Kurt Lockhart

Table of Contents

Why I'm Chatting With America

On a sunny Saturday morning, the golden retriever jumped just in time to catch the frisbee spinning across the dog park. I had recently moved to a new city and I was looking to make friends, so I stopped to ask the frisbee tosser if I could pet his dog. We chatted for a few minutes about everything and nothing, then I asked his name and told him mine.

He laughed and said, "You're not gonna believe this, but you just became the only neighbor whose name I know. And I've lived here for three years."

I laughed along with him, but inside, my stomach dropped.

He continued, saying, "I never even really talked to my neighbors until I got a dog, and even now we just talk about our dogs. I know the names of my neighbors' dogs, but I don't know my neighbors' names."

We laughed together again – that nervous, mutually assuring laugh of new acquaintances – and parted ways after shaking hands. But his words were looping in my mind. Something is rotten in the state of our conversations if we don't even know our neighbors' names. Was this a common occurrence in our country? Have we forgotten how to connect with new acquaintances?

I decided to go chatting.

What is Chatting?

Chatting is the art of getting to know someone without having an ulterior motive. There's no set guideline or agenda, but it often follows a path from fun to meaningful. It can begin with jokes and continues into explorations of another person's interests, dreams, and passions. It's not small talk, and it's not professional talk:

- Small talk is typical, inoffensive, and cyclical. You often hear this at work – topics like weather, sports, and your commute are standard fare. It's easy to get tired of this if you're not a huge fan of discussing cloud or traffic patterns. While chatting can start with small talk, it often leads somewhere more earnest, more authentic, and more real.

- Professional talk is conversation with a specific purpose. Professional talk has the stress of clarity at all costs, provision of useful information, and sentences that are succinct and efficient. There is rarely time for folksy idioms, enjoyable turns of phrase, or tangentially-related entertaining stories. While it is dangerous for your mental well-being if used in all your interactions, it's valuable in the working world to master the steps to this activity.

If either small talk or professional talk spill over into our lives too much, it can make us either bored or stressed. Chatting helps us maintain our ability to peacefully and contentedly connect with others.

Why You Should Chat

Chatting is an amazing way to really enjoy someone else's company. When I was a kid, I ran into the mom of one of my friends at the grocery store. She said, "I just had your mom over to my house and we visited all afternoon!" In my head, I was confused, thinking: "Wait, didn't she mean my mom visited her? How could she visit someone if she was at her own house?" I later discovered that "visiting" is a Southern expression for chatting. Even though my mom was the visitor, my friend's mom was also "visiting" – taking a trip via conversation through someone else's life and looking around in a friendly, tourist-y fashion. In the same way that you should visit off-the-beaten-path spots as well as the classic tourist sites, good "visits" help you learn stories from someone's past as well as the fun and somewhat "surface" level things they've been doing (new hobbies, etc.). Chatting is an amazing way to truly experience another person by "visiting" them with your conversation.

Chatting also puts people at ease through creating a space for topics that people want to talk about. A mentor once told me, "Chatting is the art of making others feel comfortable." It's not to appear more refined or polished, it's making others and yourself feel more relaxed and peaceful. My mentor suggested that it's time we kill the opening question "What do you do?" because it either gets people talking about work (which they may not enjoy or be tired of talking about since they do it all week), or it immediately puts a status difference between the two of you (e.g. if one person has a white collar job and the other person has a blue collar job). While your work and career may come up, chatting opens the door to a host of other subjects that aren't normally discussed in day-to-day life.

How To Start Chatting

Maybe you like the idea of this, but it sounds overwhelming or awkward or just a hassle. I get it! I'm not always in the mood for chatting. I often pretend to be on a very important phone call when someone on the street wants me to donate to something or sign their petition. But here are some tips if you want to give it a shot:

- Be the one to take the initiative and take a small talk conversation to a better level.
- Take it deeper, but not too quickly. Don't ask the grocery store cashier about the meaning of life! Or, at least not at the checkout counter.
- Practice unselfconsciousness and focus on the value of the other person.
- Remember that chatting should be free flowing and fun!

Chatting is a discipline to be practiced and a muscle to be exercised. Some days you just won't have it in you to go to the conversational gym. That's ok! But I promise you that if you make it a habit, you will find that chatting is important and joyful and valuable. Maybe the next time you find yourself looking at your phone or dreading another banal conversation, you'll decide to smile, and ask someone:

"Hey! Can I pet your dog?"

The Welder (Buffalo, New York)

The original Anchor Bar, located on the corner of Main and North, is the birthplace of a delicious invention called Buffalo wings. The owner during the 1960s, Teressa Bellissimo, initially offered them for free! Apparently, chicken wings used to be thrown away or used for soup before Teressa changed the game. You go, Teressa!

As I posted up at a bar stool with a plate of wings and a fat stack of napkins, the gentlemen sitting next to me said, "Excuse me, but do you know where can I get some good oysters around here?"

He was a wiry, sun-crisped man wearing a short sleeve pearl-snap button down and white-washed Wranglers. He looked somewhere between 40 and 60, and his arms were pockmarked with dozens of tiny, white burns.

I let him know that I too was not from around here, and he quickly explained his desire for oysters:

"I grew up on a thousand acres of land in southern Utah. My mother and brother still live there, along with a couple hundred cows."

"So you're a little sick of burgers?" I ventured, grinning.

His chiseled face cracked into a wide smile. "I can only eat burgers maybe twice a month. That's why tonight I'm celebrating with chicken wings and oysters."

"What are you celebrating?" I asked.

"See these burns on my arm?" he said, rolling back his shirt sleeve to reveal even more of the tiny white pockmarks. "I'm a welder. Just finished up a big job near Buffalo. It's hard work, but I make two hundred K a year."

"No way! Sign me up." I say.

"If you can stand working in the hot sun, slowly, carefully, it's a good job. Takes about 6 weeks just to build 2 miles of pipeline."

"How'd you get into that line of work?"

"My father. He taught me that retirement was a recent invention, and he worked until he was 78. I plan to follow his example. Also, working with your hands, it keeps you fit. No beer belly for me!"

We share a laugh and I ask, "What keeps you wanting to do it the rest of your life?"

"The money is good, but it took a good while for me to get where I am. I work as hard as I can, every day, to complete the contract ahead of schedule. Then, they keep hiring me and pay me even more money the next time. It's not rocket science! Also, I send my mom 500 bucks every week. I'm Navajo, and that's in our culture. It's just what you do."

He paid his bill and slipped me his card. "Look me up if you're ever in the area. We let people come camp on our land all the time. Now, I'm off to find oysters. Take care!"

He gave me a firm handshake and strode out the door, the speckled white marks on his arms glistening in the cheap bar lights.

The Golfer (Varysburg, New York)

Sometimes the best way to know someplace is to smell it. Heading east out of Buffalo on Route 20A, you have to put your windows down and take a sniff. Yes, there is the pungent sting of manure from the cow farms, but there is also the crisp smell of sweet corn and the sugary aroma of fresh maple syrup. It's an almost magical road dotted with honor-system stands of maple candy, popcorn, or firewood where you just leave the money for whatever you decide to take with you. As you coast across the smooth blacktop, you're lulled into a trance by the hum of dozens of wind turbines that dot the horizon.

A big yellow sign hollered, *Hot Breakfast!* so I pulled off the highway into a lush, secluded golf resort. I found myself wandering into a huge, log-cabin style dining room with a full buffet of pancakes, bacon, and eggs. An elderly gentlemen in a golf polo was the only other person in the room, and he nodded to me as I filled up my plate. I sat down a few chairs over from him, said hello, and we sipped coffee in silence together for a few minutes.

"New to the league?"

"Just hungry and passing through," I reply. "What league are you in?"

"Saturday golf league. We play a different course within a 60 mile radius from Buffalo every week."

"Are you from Buffalo?"

"Grew up nearby, on Grant Island, just south of Niagara Falls. It's the largest island in the world surrounded by fresh water. I've spent most of my life there, except when I was stationed at Fort Knox."

"So you were the one guarding all the gold..." I say, smiling.

He sips his coffee and snorts, "That's what they tell everyone." He leaned in towards me, a smirk on his face. "It's really all out in Denver now. But I did meet my wife when I was stationed at Knox."

"Was she from Kentucky?" I ask.

"Yes, and once I left the service and moved back here, It took 21 trips from New York to Louisville before she'd agree to marry me."

I smiled and shook my head in amusement. "Southern women, right?"

"The best kind around." He agreed. "She'll do anything for anyone, you know. She was a teacher, and retired a few years ago. But she hasn't taken a day for herself – taking care of our grandkids, helping my daughter set up her new house..."

"You're a lucky man." I say.

"Not so lucky with my tee time," he says, getting up from the table. "10:45am, so I'll be hitting the back 9 right in the heat of the damn day."

He puts on his visor and nods to me, walking out of the lodge into the hot summer day.

The Boaters (Loon Lake, New York)

You learn a lot of little facts about life by driving. Sometimes it's little things, like the arrow next to the fuel indicator on your dashboard tells you what side of the car your tank is on. And sometimes it's big things, like the fact that interesting road signs, when followed, almost always lead to interesting experiences. Whizzing along the highway at 70 miles an hour, the "Loon Lake: Next Right" sign could easily have been ignored. But I was intrigued, the name rolled off the tongue with the promise of something mysterious and beautiful. So I turned off the highway and followed the signs down a winding back road.

After visiting Loon Lake, you're gonna want to buy one of those "I LOVE NY" shirts and write "State" at the bottom. Because while half of the state does live in the Big Apple, the other half gets to enjoy some of the most beautiful rolling hills, golden farmland, and stunning sunsets that America has to offer. Loon Lake is nestled at the bottom of an enormous, shallow valley and surrounded by dozens of homes that provide stunning views of the lake out the back door and expansive views of the surrounding countryside out the front door.

I pulled down a gravel road leading to the south side of the lake, and got out of the car to dip my feet in the water. As I approached the water's edge, I wandered through a massive pack of the lake's eponymous loons. Dark feathered, these aquatic birds were the size of large duck and equipped with prodigious vocal cords which they used to express their displeasure at my presence.

At the dock of the house about 50 feet to my right, a little girl and boy paddled around in a tiny, bright yellow boat. Their parents sat on the dock behind them, crouched around the upturned motor of a gently bobbing speedboat.

"You're not a mechanic, are you?" The woman called out.

"Unfortunately, no!" I shout back. "I would probably break it even more..."

The couple laugh and stand up from their tinkering.

"How long have y'all lived here? It's a beautiful place!"

"It's my dad's place," the man says. "We've been coming here every summer with our kids for the past few years. There are a few year-rounders, but for the most part it's vacation homes. Because of that, it's often a quiet community. As you can see, we're the only ones out on the lake today!"

"What a shame!" I respond, noticing for the first time how still and quiet the water was despite the hundreds of boats encircling the lake. "If I lived here I'd be out every day!"

The couple smile, and the woman calls out to her kids to not venture too far from the dock.

"Best of luck with the boat!" I call out, and they smile and wave as I return to my car.

The Biker (Williamsport, Pennsylvania)

Heading south on U.S. Route 15, the road meets up with the beautiful, winding West Branch of the Susquehanna River around Williamsport. The river and road snake back and forth together all the way down to Harrisburg, some sort of elaborate dance planned by highway engineers that I'm not technically inclined enough to understand.

Traffic backs up before I get south of this initial meetup, so a "Scenic Overlook" sign catches my eye enough for a quick stretch break. While the view is spectacular, I'm more intrigued by the other occupants of the overlook parking lot. A burly, bearded man and a short, plump woman wave at me as they unbuckle their helmets and dismount from their Harley. I wave back.

"Lane painters!" I hear the man shout at me.

"What's that?" I say, approaching the pair.

"Goddamn lane painters." He repeats, setting his helmet down on the seat of the motorcycle. "That's what's causing the holdup."

He points back out at the road, and the three of us stare grimly at the slow creep of mostly semis and pickups that were inching along the blacktop.

"They should be finishing up in a few minutes," he continues. I notice he's wearing a shirt with a picture of Saddam Hussein and the iconic phrase "We Got Him!" emblazoned below.

The man noticed me looking at his shirt and grinned. "I served three tours in Iraq. Our boys found him hiding in a hole about as deep as you are tall." The quote comes from Paul Bremer, head of the Coalition Provisional Authority, who told a December 14th, 2003 news conference: "Ladies and gentlemen, we got him!" "This here's my wife, we just got married," he continued proudly, introducing the woman by his side. "She just moved here from Oklahoma. I've been showing her around the area for the past month or so."

"Congratulations!" I said. "Recommend any cool spots nearby to check out?"

"Well you're practically standing on top of the Home of the Little League World Series, just down the hill. Kids from Taiwan to Panama come to this tiny town in Pennsylvania to play every year."

His eyes perk up as he looks out at the emptying highway, and he grabs his wife's hand. "Coast is clear! We're off." He shakes my hand. "Safe travels, sir!"

THE SPIRIT OF VULCAN

WISE AND JVST

The Wise Pianist (Harrisburg, Pennsylvania)

The Willow Oak Building of Harrisburg, as it is now called, used to be the Pennsylvania State Lunatic Hospital and Asylum for the Insane until it was finally closed in 2006. In the early 2000s, the complex was in the midst of a transition which left half of it occupied by government workers and the other half occupied by the remaining asylum residents. A former employee swore to me that meetings would often be interrupted by patients wandering in wearing their pajamas!

But Harrisburg, capital of Pennsylvania, has more than just an interesting past and important current function. From the batting cages and mini golf on City Island to the gilded "palace of art" inside the state capitol building, Harrisburg is a gem of a city that hugs the east bank of the Susquehanna River.

Last night, I was walking around Downtown Harrisburg as the sun was setting. Down by the Susquehanna River, a drum circle had started on the banks. Runners, bikers, and roller skaters passed by, amused. Looking down State St towards the Pennsylvania State Capitol, I saw an old piano on the sidewalk, covered by a tarp. I walked up to it and started playing and singing a song I had recently written. The door to the row house I was in front of popped open, and a woman poked her head out.

"Oh, hey, you're actually good," she said, laughing.

I smiled back at her. "I took lessons for several years when I was a kid. Have you had a lot of people come play?"

"A lot of people I don't want, too few of those I'd want. I'm looking to give away that old thing to someone who loves to play. But come in, I've got something you'll appreciate as a fellow pianist."

I walked into a beautiful living room full of Parisian art, lush furnishings, and a beautiful Yamaha baby grand piano.

"This place is amazing!" I say. "How long do you plan on staying here?"

"I'm a single mother, so until my son graduates high school," she said. "I made the money for this place literally selling shoelaces. I'm also a licensed social worker in this area, and I host exchange students during the school year. But what I'm most excited about is my dream to start an Adele Tribute Show and tour around the northeast. So let's see what you can do with something that's in tune…"

I sat down at the keys and we sang our hearts out to *Someone Like You*.

We sat in silence for a while after I had finished, until she finally said, "I sit down at this piano every day and play how I'm feeling. Some days I'm sad and I peck away with slow, soft, minor chords. Other days it's happy and the house is filled with strong, joyful major chords. That's how life is. There are recurring melodies and staccato moments and unexpected chords, but it is all beautiful, no matter what."

I thanked her for letting me sing with her and walked out into the rapidly darkening night.

The Guru (Germantown, Maryland)

"I'm well aware that I'm starting the third of three chapters in my life," she says, ushering me into my room for the weekend. "And that's why I chose to be here."

Here is a 210-acre silent retreat center spread across the forest and hills of central Maryland. While it's only a forty minute drive from the nation's capital (without traffic), you won't see a single man made thing out the back window of her home. Just gently rising fields, towering oak trees, and, if you're lucky, a herd of white-tailed deer seeming to challenge you to a staring contest.

"I'd like to hear about chapters one and two," I say, setting down my things.

She smiled and sat down with me back by the back window. "Chapter one was on a farm in Iowa, in a town of about 200 people. Folks who grow up in cities may romanticize the rural life, but it wasn't always fun when you're a kid. Some nights you'd be hungry for supper and Mom would say 'Dad's gonna be out in the fields until 9, so we'll hold dinner for him.' That's just the way it was."

"What was your favorite part about that chapter?"

"Time for reflection. Even as a young child, I knew I had a higher need that most to contemplate, take a step back and enjoy the quiet and think about my life. And time and silence were in abundance when you live a mile away from any neighbors and thirty miles from the nearest city."

"I assume that's why you chose running a silent retreat center for chapter three..."

"That, and chapter two didn't give me the meaning I thought it would. I moved east to be a schoolteacher, which I did greatly enjoy. But it didn't give me the meaning I need. Here, I've gotten the chance to do everything from hosting to preaching to counseling refugees."

"Sounds amazing," I reply. "Makes me wonder why everyone my age – including me, to be fair – is in such a rush to move to big cities and work big jobs after they finish school."

"You don't have to go to law school or seminary or business school to be happy. I've done a lot of reflecting on this, and I think I've found an answer that people your age will soon find on their own. There is a pleasure to be found in the simple life. Trimming back trees, knowing which weeds to pick from the flower bed, fixing a toilet."

"Not the answers to what I wanted to be when I grow up..." I say jokingly.

She laughed and continued, "You're right, I get it. These aren't individually what people dream of doing with their lives, they aren't glamorous when taken on their own. But put them together, along with other activities where you can love and serve others, and you have a good life. Now, I'll get out of your hair to so you can have some peace and quiet!"

I thanked her, and the weekend of silence began.

The Unlikely Fighter (Arlington, Virginia)

Krav Maga was originally designed by the Israeli Defense Forces to quickly teach the simplest and most effective elements of various fighting techniques (e.g. Boxing, Judo, Karate) to new military conscripts. I signed up for a class because it was free, and I thought it would introduce me to an interesting variety of people who populated this wealthy, highly educated suburb just outside of the nation's capital.

Surprisingly, as I found out chatting with other students a few minutes before we started, the class was not populated by the assortment of white collar consultants, lobbyists, and policy wonks that I was expected. Our teacher, an Australian Army veteran turned personal trainer, paired me up with a friendly, wiry 20-something who worked by day as a substitute teacher and moonlighted as a security guard.

"First time?" he asked, grinning, as we matched up on the mat.

"Is it that obvious?" I laughed, nervously adjusting my stance in response to our Australian drill sergeant's commands.

Today's class focused on self-defense – practicing over and over again moves for recovering quickly from being pushed over or dodging a punch. It involved lots of me falling onto the mat and taking unintentional punches that I wasn't quick enough to evade.

After the class, exhausted, my partner and I crashed onto the mats and pounded water, nursing our bruises.

"So which do you like better, security guard or teacher?" I ask.

"I think I like teaching more right now because it's new. I've been working as a security guard for past few years, but I just started teaching a few months ago. Substitute teaching is its own unique challenge, because you have to command respect and attention from the students very quickly. Both jobs require rapidly assessing a situation and asserting your control. Now, I know what you're thinking...I don't look cut out for either of my jobs in that sense."

I forgot to mention – he is about 5 foot 8 and couldn't weigh more than 150 pounds.

"It's not the size of the dog in the fight, right..." I say, trying to be encouraging.

"There's a lot of fight in this dog," he replies, smiling. "When I told my friends and family I got a job as a security guard after high school, they laughed. But since then I've saved a woman getting mugged, and a little boy from being kidnapped."

"Guess they're not laughing now!"

He gives me a playful nod and flexes. "I come here every day and fight. I've always known I want to keep people safe for a living. If people don't have that, it's almost impossible for them to do anything else."

"So what drew you to learn how to fight as a way to keep people safe?"

"I was bullied as a kid. Now, coming here, taking punches, attacking...it makes you fearless. No student in my classroom, no shady character walking by a store I'm guarding can scare me. So that's why I fight."

The Historian (Johnson City, Tennessee)

Not many people know that the chorus and melody of Old Crow Medicine Show's "Wagon Wheel" was actually written by Bob Dylan. Dylan's original was never officially released, and the bootleg version (known as "Rock Me, Mama") inspired homesick Ketch Secor of Old Crow Medicine Show to write the verses that reference a journey home which passes through Johnson City, Tennessee. As I drove south from Virginia towards Asheville, I stopped at the city's downtown and asked a man about the connection with the famous country song.

"We've been famous since way before that song, brother. Infamous, more like it..." the man replied. "In the 1920s and 30s Johnson City (he pronounced it "Johns-zity") was known as 'Little Chicago' because Al Capone used to stop here. This was the speakeasy of the South!"

"Whoa! What brought him all the way here from Chicago?" I asked.

"Well he was in town a lot, and it was about half way on the way to Florida. So it became a stopping place. I'll show you his main spot down here real quick."

My guide let me around the corner to an imposing Italian style building.

"This was the hotel he used to stay at! I don't know if he was smuggling drugs or what. They've ripped up some old buildings around the corner and there were underground tunnels underneath the bar he used to sit at and have drinks. Let me show you!"

Again I followed my guide on this impromptu historical tour, and we stood in front of a Chicago-style speakeasy with a big sign above it – "Capone's!"

"And I remember when I was a kid this place was mean." The man said, reminiscing. "Cops were mean. It was rough around here. So I guess you could say his legacy lived on here in Little Chicago."

"What do you do here now? I asked.

"I work with the young professionals of this city during the day. And in the evenings I work in home security. I grew up here and it's good to see the city growing. Medical field taking off. The university here is trying to turn this into a college campus feel – and that will really help downtown business."

"What a place!" I said. "Way more than just a catchy-sounding location for a song."

"The song was good for us though. We get a lot of folks hitchhiking through, and I guess the Old Crow fellow was one of them." The man grinned and shook my hand. "Any publicity is good publicity, right?"

CASH ONLY

Welcome to the BUS

ATTENTION
THIS IS A PLACE OF BUSINESS
PATIO, BUS & ALL
SEATING ARE FOR
CUSTOMERS ONLY

Get on the bus

_sh Only
_Seating -
_nd Inside
_s is for
_rs O_

The Homesick Glassblower (Asheville, North Carolina)

Tourists snap pictures of a man with a feather in his man bun and a snake wrapped around his shoulders. Breweries and coffee shops are packed with the tattooed and the pierced who come to savor the fresh air, the mountain views, and the safety offered by the hipster haven of the South. One such brewery sports a double purpose – walking inside the door you are greeted with a dazzling variety of glassware. As you walk towards the back, you see a small bar to the left and a glassblowing furnace to your right. Patrons sip from a local brew and look on as glass is heated to over 2,400 degrees Fahrenheit. The glass blowers then use the blowpipe to shape the molten hot white material, cool it in a variety of buckets, then set down the finished product to cool in front of an admiring crowd.

I approach the bar and nod to the older gentleman who is trading good-natured insults with the much younger glass blowers about the quality of their products.

"Do you guys take turns bartending and glassblowing?" I ask as I sit down.

"I help out glassblowing whenever they need it," he says. "Which is more often than I'd like. They're still learning!"

"How long have you been in Asheville?"

"I grew up here. Went off to University of Georgia, and then went hitchhiking around the country in '84."

"I'm doing something similar!" I reply. " Luckily, I'm borrowing my brother's car. Any crazy stories from the road?"

"We had a guy pick us up, then buy liquor on the Texas-Oklahoma border. We stopped at a McDonalds and he goes to the bathroom for a really long time. Finally, we bust in and find him passed out with an empty fifth of Jack lying next to him and wads of bills falling out of his pockets. I'll admit, it was a moral dilemma for me as to what I should do. Found a phone number is his wallet, and I called it from a pay phone. It was his sister – so I drove him to her house which was about an hour away. She gave me dinner and a bed for the night, then arranged a free ride for me to California with her friend. Guess it pays to do the right thing!"

"Sometimes…" I grin. "I think you got lucky that the sister was nearby."

"True," he responds. "I've been lucky my whole life. I worked in IT at the South Pole for 12 years – had to stand in front of a 'Happy Light' that simulated sunshine every morning. First I worked deep at the center with astrophysicists – they weren't much fun. Then I got stationed out with the biologists toward the coast – they would take me out to see the penguins and the seals and the killer whales. THAT was the best time of my life. Every morning you got to see a zoo in your front yard."

"That's amazing!" I said. "What brought you back here?"

"Asheville's home," he replied simply. "At some point, everybody has to head on home."

BIRTHPLACE OF
ELVIS PRESLEY

Elvis Aaron Presley was bor
Jan. 8, 1935, in this hous
built by his father. Presley
career as a singer and enter
tainer redefined America
popular music. He died Aug. 1
1977, at Memphis, Tennesse

The Lawyer (Tupelo, Mississippi)

"That's my uncle, standing next to Elvis!" He says, pointing at one of the signed pictures that covered the walls of the diner. "I'm fourth generation Tupelo, and it's a small enough town that everybody pretty much knew everybody."

I had visited Tupelo to see the birthplace of Elvis Presley, and I ended up stopping at a small diner across the street afterwards. While the omnipresent Elvis decorations suggested this might be a tourist trap, the handful of other patrons looked like locals. Sitting a few bar stools over from me was a middle aged man in a suit, who nodded at me as I sat down.

"It's a hot day for a suit," I say.

"You're telling me!" He laughs. "I'm a lawyer, and I have a trial in Oxford I just came from."

"I'm heading there next to visit Ole Miss! I'm on a road trip around America."

"My daughters would love to do that after they graduate! They are both there now, and I went to Ole Miss for undergrad and law school. We used to tailgate there every home football game, but now the traffic backs up almost all the way here sometimes. Glad you stopped through Tupelo though!"

"Did you hear any stories about Elvis from your family who knew him?"

"A few, but none better than the famous ones. For example, one day his mom took him to the Tupelo general store to get him a birthday present. He wanted a .22 rifle, but his mom thought it was too dangerous. So, unhappily, he settled for a guitar – and the world will be forever grateful he did!"

"Amazing." I replied. "Well I better hit the road to Oxford – what's the best way there?"

"Don't listen to this suit," remarked an older man good-naturedly to the lawyer, laughing and slapping him on the back as he passed by.

The older man and the lawyer argued good-naturedly for a few minutes over which route was the fastest to Oxford. I was amazed at this – my generation simply puts something in Google Maps or Waze and sets out. For them, it was an opportunity to chat and discuss.

"Safe travels," said the lawyer, and grabbed my check off the table as I was getting up to go. "Your lunch is on me!"

The Plantation Owners (Scott, Arkansas)

"We have ghosts here, you know," said the woman matter-of-factly, gesturing around the stately mansion. I felt like I had stepped into an untouched relic of the American south, a plantation home on the Arkansas Delta built in the 1880s.

"Over 30 rooms in this house, and we mainly just use the one." She gestures to her husband, seated next to her on an opulent couch in the entry hall. "So there's plenty of room for them to run around at night."

"Have the ghosts ever talked to you?" I asked.

"They whisper," chimes in her husband, speaking with great intensity. "The main one is named Isaac. He leaves his boots by the fireplace some nights."

"I think he knocked over some potted plants upstairs last night," states the wife knowingly, nodding at her husband. "He's just testing us, though!"

She laughs, and smiles reassuringly at me.

"We only moved in a few months ago, and he's seeing what the new owners are made of!"

"What inspired you all to move into a historic home like this?" I asked.

"On a Friday, we went out for a drive on a dirt road with a pack of wine coolers," said the husband, brushing back his thick grey hair. "On a Sunday, we signed the lease!"

I had so many more questions, but my ride was about to leave and I didn't want to be trapped for the night in a house full of ghosts.

"Thanks for stopping by!" called out the plantation owners, waving from the massive front porch as I walked towards the road.

What nice people, I thought. I hope Isaac takes a liking to them too!

The Big Texan (Amarillo, Texas)

"I've tried it twice, believe me. It's bested me."

The man was sprawled out at one of the ring of upper level tables that overlook the eater's stage, tucking into a massive plate of steak and heaping sides. We're at a restaurant called The Big Texan, an iconic Route 66 stop that offers a free 72oz steak. Yes, you read that right, free! The billboards advertising this offer dot the highway from hundreds of miles away, so I had to stop in and check out whether this was really true. Here's the catch – you have to eat it in an hour, along with a shrimp cocktail, baked potato, salad, and roll. If you complete it, you get the steak for free and a t-shirt for bragging rights. If you don't complete it, you have to pay the $72 price of the meal...but, you get a t-shirt that says you tried!

The attempters are put on a big, elevated stage in the middle of the restaurant, with huge 60 minute digital timers peering down at them from above. Like the gladiators of old, you test your abilities alone in the arena, in front of an often encouraging, sometimes jeering crowd of captivated onlookers.

"Third time's the charm, right? Why not try one last time?" I ask the man sitting next to me, who explained the rules of the challenge.

"No way – I'm a local. It was enough to be embarrassed twice in front of people I grew up with who work here. I grew up coming here as a kid all the time, watching people from all over the world try their luck at this. And only about 1 in 5 normally get it, if that."

"So what was your approach for Attempt #2 vs. Attempt #1? What did you change?"

"The first time, I focused just on the steak. I ate the whole thing."

"So you did do it!?" I ask, incredulously. "You've won the challenge!!"

"No, no, no," he says, wagging his finger at me. "You didn't let me finish. You have to eat the sides – all of them. I took one bite of the mashed potatoes, and realized that if I took a second bite I would send that whole steak right back up in front of all these nice people. All these kids, tourists, whoever... they didn't need to see that. So I tapped out. The second time, I started with the sides. But then I couldn't even get halfway done with the steak."

"Hey, I'm impressed you even tried. But you still like coming here?"

"Of course, the steaks are amazing!" he says, gesturing down at his plate. "This one here's just an 18 ounce, only a quarter of the size of the big kahuna."

He grins at me and points down to the stage. "Besides, it's a great price for dinner and a show!"

The Retirees (Capulin, New Mexico)

The one mile trail winds around the 8000 foot high rim of the Capulin Volcano, providing views of New Mexico, Texas, Oklahoma, Colorado, and even Kansas. From the snowcapped mountains in the north to the rolling grasslands to the south, you feel like Simba surveying the pride lands...except everything the light touches belongs to someone else.

The drive up from the base of the extinct volcano is harrowing enough, winding along a narrow road with nothing to the right separating you from oblivion. When I reached the top, an older couple was just coming finishing up their loop hike.

"Good thing you're young!" said the man, who took a seat on the stone wall overlook next to me. "The altitude is a doozy!"

"You're a doozy," said the woman to her husband good-naturedly. "The views are so nice though!"

"Any chance you're from Michigan?" I ask, picking up on her accent.

"How did you know?" The woman said, baffled. She inspected her clothing to make sure no logos had given her away. "Our plates are New Mexico!"

"The way you said nice." I laughed. "And it was a lucky guess!"

"She's actually a speech pathologist," her husband said. "So you've impressed her."

"My favorite accent is old Virginia, around the Tidewater region," she told me. "They still preserve the deep accents of Old English speech, it's incredible."

"What brings y'all here?" I ask.

"We've retired here, actually," he said. "My grandfather was from this area – he actually is in a picture over there on that historic marker, working on building the road up this mountain."

"He's a braver man than I," I say. "Just driving it was scary enough."

"It was during the Great Depression, and a Civil Works Project was approved here under FDR's program. He was just happy to have a job!"

"Well drive safe heading down!" I say, as they get into their old Ford pickup.

"She gets a nice view out the passenger window..." He grumbled amiably, starting the engine.

"...While he gets to cling desperately to the wheel!" she chuckled, elbowing him in the stomach.

He rolls his eyes as she pecks him on the cheek, and away they go.

YELLOWSTONE NATIONAL PARK TRANSPORTATION

The Preservationist (Cheyenne, Wyoming)

"I'm supposed to be playing golf in Tampa right now," he chuckled, adjusting the rimless glasses that had fallen down his nose. "But this opportunity was too good to pass up."

This opportunity is restoring the Wyoming State Capitol building, which he points out to me across the street from the Wyoming State Museum. It's covered in scaffolding, but you can tell it is a majestic old building from the 19th century. Wyoming has always been one of the most interesting states to me – the least populated in the nation, but full of some of the most beautiful natural wonders such as the Grand Tetons and Yellowstone. The museum we're standing in has some relics from the early settlers who came out here, such as the stagecoaches that were used to take wealthy visitors around the parks over a hundred years ago.

"I began my career as an Army medic," he begins, as I ask him how he came across this opportunity. He pulls out a yellowed military identification card.

"This says it expires in 1972!" I say, pointing out the date.

"Doesn't matter," he laughed. "I always keep this in my wallet, because they respect veterans out here! Anyways, after I got out of the service I got into historic preservation. I absolutely loved it, but during the 90s when I saw what was going on in Kosovo, I went over there to serve in the Peace Corps. Since then, I've done tours with the Peace Corps in three other countries around the world."

"So what brought you back to the States?"

"Well, my partner and I wanted to retire. We had a house bought in Tampa, everything. Then I got a call from an old colleague who described the renovations planned for the capitol...and I bought the plane ticket to Wyoming that night."

"How did your partner react?"

"That phone call was a tough one, but he was ok with it since we're just here temporarily," he laughs, scratching his head. "But we'll be done restoring the capitol in 2019. Then off to Florida for my daily tee time!"

The Truck Driver (Little America, Wyoming)

Almost 1% of the United State population are truck drivers. Big rigs, 18-wheelers, semis, whatever you call them…their drivers sit for long hours behind a wheel, often alone, bringing to us the stuff we need and use every day. Federal rules are very specific for them, mandating that they only drive 11 hours within a 14 hour window. After that, they must take a 10 hour break. While the premise behind this law makes sense – to ensure that our nation's roads are safe and that these drivers are well rested – truckers get paid by the mile. Things like traffic jams, which are just inconveniences to the rest of us, can mean a rapidly shrinking paycheck as their hours are eaten up while their truck stands still.

Trucks are my main company as I whiz across I-80, a lonely highway that whips across long, empty stretches of the southern half of Wyoming. About three quarters of the way across the state, I spot a billboard advertising 75 cent ice cream cones at a place called Little America. I had no choice but to stop.

Built in 1952, this Little America is the original of a chain of four hotels. It once had the world's largest filling station (55 pumps!) and used a penguin to advertise, a play on the similarities between its isolated location in the middle of Wyoming and the remoteness of Antarctic exploration stations of the 1950s that were also called Little America.

As I enjoy breakfast for dinner in the hotel's cafe, an older woman raises the blinds on the western side of the building to let in a gorgeous sunset.

"This is nothing! You should see the sunrise out here," she exclaims as she walks by, noticing my jaw dropping as I gaze out the window.

"Incredible. How long have you been out here?" I ask.

"I grew up Wyoming, but I used to work as a truck driver until my husband had a heart attack 5 years ago."

"I'm sorry to hear that," I say.

"He's still alive, thanks to God and Social Security Disability. He was out here chasing oil rigs, but now we've settled down a few miles from here and I found this job."

"What's it like living somewhere so remote?"

"People like it here. We have a lady in housekeeping who's worked here for 57 years. The problem is it's getting too big here."

"Really?" I chuckle, gesturing around the vast emptiness that surrounds the hotel.

"You'd be surprised," she laughs, wiping down the table next to me. "Also, I don't like crowds. We used to live two hours north of here, up over the mountains. But it got too big."

"Don't ever head East," I warn her, smiling.

"Oh I won't, honey, trust me. When it finally does get too big here I'll move somewhere else! There's lots of room out here for people like me."

The Missionary (Salt Lake City, Utah)

While the Civil War was raging off to the East, a temple unlike anything America had ever seen was slowly but surely being erected far to the West. Fleeing persecution in Illinois, the Mormon prophet Brigham Young arrived in the Salt Lake valley and determined the location of the temple in 1847. While he would not see its completion, the temple finally opened in 1893. Only Mormons can enter the temple itself, but the grounds surrounding it draw tourists from around the world to marvel at the structure.

Non-Mormons are allowed to attend Sunday services, which are held in other locations for each particular "ward" (a grouping based on geographic location). I decided to venture into one, and stopped to chat with a young 20-something guy who was arranging pieces of bread and tiny water cups at a table near the entrance.

"Hey man, welcome!" he says, smiling. "Are you new to the ward?"

"Yes!" I say, unsure whether to reveal my status as both an outsider to their ward and to their religion. "I'm traveling around the country and writing about interesting people and places that I find."

"Well it's the same here as your ward back home..." he laughs.

"This is actually my first time at a Mormon service!" I admit.

"No way!" He looks genuinely astonished. "I totally thought you were Mormon, L.O.L." (To clarify, he actually spells out the letters of the acronym)

"Sorry to disappoint..." I grin.

"I just got back from mission – I was in Mexico for two years. I'm 21 now, and starting my first year at Brigham Young University."

"Wow, what was your favorite part of your mission?"

"We had these two kids who lived about 4 miles from downtown. Their parents would give them money every day to take the bus in to school. They decided to save their bus money and walk to school every day, and they used what they had saved to help the poor in their neighborhood. It really inspired me to sacrifice more to serve the church, after seeing their example."

The service is about to start, and he finishes his preparations with the bread and water.

"Well, I have to help give out the elements, but I will come sit with you after that."

He shakes my hand and smiles, and I take a seat in a nearby pew. I've been to many different types of church services in my life, but never before have I been welcomed so warmly. I get a strange feeling as I watch him serve the elements to the congregation - he is so similar to me, that's it's almost like I'm seeing myself put pieces of bread on a tray and fill tiny cups of water. And, maybe he would have been me, and I would have been him, if somehow our families had swapped us at birth.

The missionary makes good on his offer to sit with me a few minutes into the service, and, just like that, I've made a new friend.

The Barista and the Bartender (Tetonia, Idaho)

"Enjoy our little slice of heaven!" reads the Idaho Airbnb description, and boy, is she right. While this state may be famous for its potatoes, the views heading north from Utah are simply astonishing. As you cruise through a fairly flat, grassy valley, the Grand Tetons shoot up to the east. The morning sunrise peeks over these towering mountains that seem to come out of nowhere.

At a cafe nearby, a couple sits on barstools and eat breakfast. There is something shockingly peaceful about their demeanor, something so laid back and at ease that almost forget to smile back as I grab a stool near them.

"From Virginia?" the man asks, nodding to my car outside. "You're a long ways from home."

"The car's from there, but I'm from Texas...still, yes, a long ways from home." I say, noticing the only other car in the lot has a North Carolina license plate. "What brings y'all out here?"

"We come here every year, after the summer rush is over," the woman explains. "We own a coffee shop slash bar in the Outer Banks. I'm the barista, and he's the bartender. We like to escape out here to a family cabin after the beach traffic slows down."

"That's a nice approach to life. Seasonal – you work hard for a while, then relax hard for a while."

"Exactly!" The man replies. "I go out to Yellowstone every day that I can to go fly fishing."

"And I like to actually explore the park..." she laughs, elbowing the bartender. "Rather than sit at a desk and read about them like I used to."

"What do you mean?" I ask.

"I used to work for the Park Service. Funny enough, I never actually set foot in a park as part of my job. I just helped manage operations from an office."

"You're kidding me!?" I reply. "That must have been aggravating...so close, but yet so far."

"I know, right," she laughs. "I respect the people who can do it, but not me."

"We deal with tourists who complain to us all summer, even though they're on vacation," he says. "It's unbelievable. But it's worth it, because we get to be in this the other half of the year."

"We've tried the typical 9-5 path and it's not for us," she says. "Everyone can make their own choices, but at least for us, this is a better life!"

The Accidental Skinnydipper (Pray, Montana)

Just north of Yellowstone National Park, the Chico Hot Springs provide guests with pure, chemical-free water that varies in heat from day to day depending on geothermal activity. Most of those lounging in the pool this afternoon seem to be locals, and the members of the crowd that happen to be facing the entrance to the men's locker room die laughing as an older gentlemen makes it almost out of the dressing room without his swimsuit on. He stops himself just in time, turns heel back into the dressing room, and re-emerges a few seconds later properly suited up.

His wife, who he joins in the pool, turns an even deeper shade of red as he calls out good-naturedly to the crowd… "You forget sometimes when you're so in love!" She blushes and laughs, despite herself, as he grabs her hand after his public address.

I'm sitting nearby in the pool, and I nod and smile at them as they float near.

"It's her birthday today too!" he informs me, slapping his forehead with the palm of his hand. "And we're supposed to eat dinner at this club tonight."

"Don't worry," I say. "You managed to stop yourself just in time…"

"Thank God," he says, laughing. He picks up a lightweight, volleyball sized bouncy ball and tosses it to his wife. They proceed to bump it back in forth with greater skill and speed than I would have imagined for folks their age. "Would you like to join us?"

"Sure!" I reply. "If you can give me some tips for exploring Yellowstone?"

"Stay away from the buffalo," his wife advises, passing the ball to me. Between the three of us, we do our best to keep the ball aloft for as many touches as possible.

He jumps in to explain her comment, "One day I was swimming in the Boiling River near the north entrance, and I go to the ledge to pull myself out onto the grass. I stop myself with my eyes about an inch over the edge of the river bank, and I see an eye ten times the size of mine looking straight back. I slowly settle back down into the water, and an enormous buffalo just eases himself over the edge and plops into the water next to me. I lay still for a few minutes, and finally the buffalo finishes splashing around in the shallow water and takes off."

He grabs the ball in the air and looks me right in the eye.

"If I pulled myself up one second faster I wouldn't be here now. The buffalo would've gored my face off, just like that."

He passed the ball back to his wife, and we continue the game with contented focus for a while. The accidental skinnydipper dives long for the ball after I accidentally tap it way too hard, but he misses. He shrugs his shoulders and laughs.

"One of the greatest joys in life is going for it, all the way, even if you fail." He grabs his wife's hand. "C'mon honey, it's time for your birthday dinner."

STARBUCKS

COFFEE · TEA · SPICES

LATTE

ITS DEFENDERS WI

The Reluctant Vegan (Seattle, Washington)

"COLD, TROLLED HALIBUT!!!"

The ponytailed man in a Seahawks jersey yells as he swings back the 50 pound fish, and then throws it with all his might.

"COLD, TROLLED HALIBUT!!!"

The man behind the counter calls in response, and manages to catch the flying fish like a football.

The crowd goes wild.

We are at the Pike Place Market in Seattle, one of the oldest continually operated markets in America. The flying fish tradition draws tourists to watch customers' orders go sailing from their display stand to behind the counter for wrapping. From fresh cut flowers to cold, trolled halibut – this market has everything you could want and more. Across the street, an older gentleman in a Navy Uniform serenades the line to order from the Original Starbucks.

Down the steps in an alley below the market, the notorious Gum Wall (in response to a sign that once read "Please Do Not Stick Gum Here") features messages, designs, and original works of art made entirely out of chewing gum. A man skips down Pike Street dressed in full medieval jester garb. I ask a friend if this is for Halloween – he responds – "No, it's just Seattle."

I happen to stop in front of a vegan stand in the market, and the cashier gives me a friendly smile.

"Do you have to be a vegan to work here?" I ask, grinning.

"No, but it helps!" he says. "At first I just tried it because my girlfriend insisted. It was tough at first, but now I love it!"

"Really?" I ask, looking around. "You're not just saying that because she's here…"

"I mean it! She's at work," he says. "I used to like to hunt deer. Now I just eat what the deer eat."

"What about all the amazing foods you miss, like pizza?"

"Try our cashew cheese pizza. It'll change your life."

The Meticulous Artist (Portland, Oregon)

The cafe at Powell's Books is quiet, and dozens of bicycles are lined up in a row outside the big glass windows. Bearded, beanied patrons sip espresso while flipping through used books. In the midst of all this, an artist is at work. His creations are intricately designed, botanically correct flowers made of nothing but industrial grade paper towels. Headphones in, he bobs to the music while nimbly arranging and twisting the scraps of paper strewn across the table.

"Which flower do you like the best?"

He caught me staring, and his question refers to the three flowers displayed at the front of his table.

"The rose." I say, following my gut.

"Correct," he says. "I make three types of flowers – the morning glory, the lily, and the rose. About 80% of men choose the rose – it's hardwired in nature."

"What do you mean?"

"Art is just a mixture of our mating and hunting instincts. I use math to make art that is pleasing to the eye, and the rose is what does it for men. Do you know the Fibonacci sequence?"

"The last time I took math was high school…"

"It's 1, 1, 2, 5, 8, 13, and on and on it goes. It's found everywhere in nature, and I use it to choose the right number for outer leaves, supporting leaves, and the reproductive system."

"How did you learn how to do this?"

"There's book 1, book 2, and book 3," He says, gesturing to the three flowers.

"So you would say you 'wrote the book' on paper flowers…" I say, smiling.

"Precisely. My paper towel of choice is the Tork Premium MB570."

"And Powell's is cool with you setting up shop here?"

"I've come here every day for over three years. I've had NBC, ABC, and PBS all sit at that table right there and watch. I've lost track of how many mayors have sat where you're sitting. They understand that's what art should be – bringing beauty to people in places where they go every day."

The Betrothed (Crater Lake, Oregon)

The entire trip would have been worth it to experience this moment.

On Halloween afternoon, I was walking along the West Rim Drive of Crater Lake. This was the last day this section of the road around the lake was open to the public before it closed for the winter. Crater Lake was formed about 7,000 years ago when a volcano collapsed, and it is the clearest, purest, and (if the park ranger I talked to is correct) tastiest freshwater body in the world.

As I walked along the path, I saw an older man taking a picture of an older woman with the lake in the background. While this would have been nothing out of the ordinary on its own, I was intrigued by the woman's classic "she said yes!" pose, the one that involves prominently displaying a wedding band on the left ring finger.

"He just proposed!" she called out to me as I pass by.

I stop, and say congratulations. I smile at the man as he finishes taking the picture. "What a great place to pop the question, it is so beautiful out here!"

"It's her favorite place in the world," he says, and the couple embrace.

"How did y'all meet?" I ask.

I can tell immediately that this question will not be answered with some standard response like at church or at a party.

"My wife passed away a little over a year ago," said the man. "I'd been happily married to her for 40 years."

"She was my best friend in the world," said the woman. "We grieved for her together."

Gesturing to the woman, he said, "She'd known my family for years, she knows my kids, she knows my grandkids. A few months ago, we started to realize that maybe there was more to this than just friends helping each other cope."

"I've been single for 30 years," said the woman. "Waiting for the right guy to come along. There's been a lot of skunks along the way, let me tell you!"

"And here I was, right under your nose," said the man. "And it took this tragic loss to bring us together."

"What an incredible story," I say. "Best wishes to you both. Any advice for a young guy looking to find someone to marry?"

"You gotta find the trifecta," said the man. "A good heart, a sense of humor, and – most importantly – love for God."

"Do you know the old saying – when the student is ready, the teacher appears?" asked the woman. "It's the same way for love. When you are ready to get married, the right person will be in the right place at the right time."

She laughs, and the couple embraces again.

"Hopefully it won't be 30 years for you!

BOARDMART

1261 MARKET ST

243-2323
243-7669 (SNOW)

The Believer (Redding, California)

Imagine a town where 10% of the population attends the same church every week. I was astonished by this statistic, but when I crunched the numbers it turns out to be fairly accurate – Redding has about 90,000 people and Bethel Church has about 9,000 attendees each week. This non-denominational, charismatic mega church has received much scrutiny over the years, but I'll limit my thoughts to what I learned from a coffee shop chat that turned into an hour long conversation about life, faith, and the reality of miracles.

The 20-something lady was sitting at the table next to me, her Bible open as she carefully wrote a few words in her journal.

"This is a random guess, but are you part of that big church in this town?"

"How did you know?" she responds wryly. It's clear she's gotten this question before. "I guess that's what I signed up for when I moved here."

"What brought you to Redding?"

"God told me to move here from LA to be a part of the church – I was a student for a few years in the Bethel School of Supernatural Ministry."

"Wow, what a title!" I say, smiling. "I want to see that framed diploma."

She laughs and continues, "It's unaccredited, more of an equipping program for people to learn about experiencing God and bringing healing to the world."

"Have you had an opportunity to put those skills to use?"

"Funny you should ask…exactly a year ago from today, I was working as a waitress when a woman fell on the floor, choking. My manager ran over and tried the Heimlich, but it didn't work. She started to turn purple and red and her whole face and neck swelled up. An off duty nurse came over and checked her pulse, and said she was dead. I did a ride along with an officer back in LA and I saw a dead person then, so I know what they look like. This lady was gone. But then I heard God say 'Put your hand on her head and pray.' I was scared, because I was an employee in uniform and I knew there could be legal ramifications with this poor lady passing away in our restaurant. But I heard God say it again, so I did it."

"Wow. What did the voice sound like?"

"I pray all the time, but I'd never heard it like this before – just quiet, but firm, just for me to hear. So I did it. I said 'Jesus, bring her back'. And her lips turned from a cold purple back to red. I said it again, 'Jesus, bring her back.' And she started to breathe. Her chest was going up and down and the swelling went down and her face went back to its normal color. By the time the ambulance arrived and tried to put the oxygen on her, she was back on her feet. She was going on about how her throat hurt but otherwise she was fine."

"Incredible. How full was the restaurant? Did anybody try to film it?"

"I think it was a sacred moment. That ordinary restaurant of 30 or 40 people just quietly eating hamburgers became a holy place. No one thought to take out their phone, everyone was just in awe of what God was doing. I actually ran into someone from the restaurant a month ago and they had become a Christian that same day!"

The Wine Cyclist (Napa, California)

"The fires here weren't my first brush with death," he said, long rows of vines flying by on either side of us as we bike along the dirt road. "I've been a very lucky man."

"How close was your apartment to the October fires?"

"I was asleep, and my girlfriend kept calling me and calling me. The Tubbs fire started on a Sunday night, and it traveled over 10 miles in just a few hours. The fire alarms didn't go off in my building, because the fires were so far away at first. I finally woke up, and I saw the fires out the window. I put on my basketball shorts, grabbed my dog, and jumped in the car. The smoke was so thick I could barely see, and I was coughing and speeding down the wrong side of the road. I felt the heat of the fires – I was literally seconds away from death. I managed to drive to a hospital and they put the oxygen mask on me."

"Wow. And here you are a few weeks later, leading a bike tour of the Napa Valley. You know how to bounce back!"

"I love my job. I get to meet people from around the world, drink wine, and stay in shape by biking and kayaking. No fire is gonna keep me from doing that."

"You are a lucky man! You said you had another brush with death?"

"When I was 16 my car went off the road near the top of that cliff over there. I thought I was going over. Something told me to unbuckle my seatbelt, hop into the passenger seat, and open the door. I was about to just jump for it before the car went over, then it hit a bump and it changed directions to stay on the cliff. I crashed into a tree and a huge branch went right through the front windshield into the driver's seat. If I had stayed where I was, I would have been decapitated."

"Why do you think these kinds of things have happened to you? Not many people can say they cheated death twice."

"I really couldn't say. I don't know why. But I do know how it's changed me. My girlfriend hates me sometimes because she says I always wake up happy. She hasn't even had her coffee yet and I'm just beaming. Every morning, I'm just happy to be alive."

The Ranger (Tehachapi, California)

"Si, se puede!"

This iconic motto of the United Farm Workers was developed during one of the many hunger fasts Cesar Chavez did to protest unjust working conditions. His most famous efforts include the 5-year Delano Grape Strike (calling for a nationwide boycott of grapes) and advocacy for the California Agricultural Labor Relations Act (the first state law to allow collective bargaining for farm workers). In 2008, an English translation of the motto was popularized when adopted as Barack Obama's campaign slogan – Yes, We Can!

A friendly park ranger at The Cesar Chavez National Monument showed me the original office which houses his furnishing and artifacts.

"I love working here!" she said, pointing to a picture of the man. "He was one of the greats of nonviolent activism – we need more people like him today."

"What are the most important things we can learn from his example?"

"You have to combine great communication with great morals. He had the ability to write and speak in a way that people would listen to, and he followed up this words with sacrificial actions."

"Like the hunger strikes?" I ask.

"Yes. In fact my favorite quote of his comes from the end of the 1968 fast. It was huge public event that all kinds of big shots showed up to attend. Cesar Chavez was too weak to give the speech he had prepared, so it was read for him."

I thanked her for her time, and stopped to read the entire quote. Outside the window, I looked out at the grave of this man that lies next to his wife in a peaceful garden. The words he said almost 50 years ago still shake my heart today:

"When we are really honest with ourselves we must admit that our lives are all that really belong to us. So it is how we use our lives that determines what kind of men we are. It is my deepest belief that only by giving our lives do we find life. I am convinced that the truest act of courage, the strongest act of manliness is to sacrifice ourselves for others in a totally nonviolent struggle for justice. To be a man is to suffer for others. God help us to be men!"

The Friendly Brit (Las Vegas, Nevada)

"You can do anything you want here!"

Red faced and ecstatic, the British man booms this like a proverb as he furiously cast bright pink chips across the roulette table. It's 2am in the casino and the party shows no sign of slowing down. A bachelorette party shrieks from a nearby craps table. Across the ornate golden entry hall, a bride in a long white wedding dress drops it low to an Usher song.

"I've lived everywhere in the world, and nothing compares to here. I'm from London, but I worked in China for 20 years and Australia for 10."

"What makes this place so special to you?"

"There are no rules in Vegas." He lights a Marlboro from the pack lying next to his gin and tonic. "You can drink at the table, smoke at the table. Anything you can dream of you can do here."

A group of Japanese businessmen approaches our table, and I watch in awe as they lay down Benjamin after Benjamin. The dealer pushes the tallest stack of chips I've ever seen across the green felt. The roulette ball drops onto 18, and the Brit goes wild as he collects his winnings.

"And best of all, no one judges you!" he continues, sliding all his winnings onto Red. "It's the best place in the world. Now c'mon, look at the past few numbers. Red is hot."

I slide my chips onto Red too and clink my glass with the Brit.

"Here goes nothing!" I laugh, and watch the ball slide around and around as the wheel spins. The Japanese businessman next to me smiles and nods at us as he places his chips on Red as well. No words are needed at the casino – we are all in this together. The House may have the advantage, but we have the team spirit.

The ball lingers on the lip of the wheel then drops, bouncing, skirting across the Red and Black and Green numbers as Japanese, British, and American men all join together to hope, and pray...

It lands on a Red, and we all go absolutely nuts.

Welcome to fabulous Las Vegas.

The Producer (Zion National Park, Utah)

I didn't expect to see a man in a chicken mask near the end of the 15-mile Zion Canyon. After entering the park from the south, you wind your way up the canyon by foot or by shuttle until you reach the Narrows. There, you leave behind the dry path and continue in the river through the...you guessed it...very narrow section of the canyon as far as you dare.

Many hikers lurk at the entrance to the Narrows after coming up the canyon, watching who dares to venture further up. Those who do often come equipped with thick pants, waterproof shoes, and walking sticks. All of us at the entrance to the canyon stop to watch a man, alone, wearing only shorts and Crocs, boldly walk on ahead. It was then that I saw him put an elaborate chicken mask on and pose for a picture in front of the Narrows entrance.

"What's the story on the mask?" I ask.

"I'm a producer!" He removes the mask and smiles. "I make beats, mostly for hip hop or for YouTube videos. The mask started as a joke with my boys about 8 years ago, but now it's my calling card."

"I used to be a mascot. I get the allure of putting something on and becoming someone new!"

"For sure man! I take pictures with it wherever I go. I normally travel to parks and stuff by day and spin beats by night."

"That sounds like the dream. Who do you like working with better, hip hop or YouTube clients?"

"Hip hop, hands down. Everyone in hip hop is nice. YouTube celebrities, not so much. They started out as just regular people but then they got a couple million views, and the fame goes to their heads. They think they're too cool to talk to you."

I looked him up later and found out that he actually had a couple of million views on one of his solo tracks. Guess the fame doesn't go to everyone's heads!

The Horse Tamer (Monument Valley, Arizona)

"They come here under The Big Hogan to discern the future."

The enormous hole on the top of the mesa's half dome formation looks like an eye peering down on me, my Navajo guide, and our two horses.

"We call it that because it is shaped like the Hogan, the traditional home of our people. So those who live in the valley come here for refuge. They light a fire here and our holy people look ahead at what is to come."

Popularized by John Wayne westerns such as The Searchers, we are riding deep into the heart of Monument Valley. The rugged, arid beauty of this place is made more vivid to me by its quiet and stillness. We trot past rock formations with names like The Three Sisters, Rain God Mesa, and The Sun's Eye. I took a bumpy Jeep ride down from the entrance to the stables, past where is accessible to folks in vehicles on the self-guided loop of the northern half of the valley.

"You ready to gallop?" My guide grins at me. "We've got to get back before dark."

My guide takes off with his horse across the plain as the sun begins dipping below the horizon. My horse, Spud, is not quite as eager to follow – so I settle for a slightly quickened trot. While dozens of Navajo (they call themselves Diné, meaning "The People") still live in this valley, we don't see another soul as we quietly pad past petroglyphs and buttes. I feel like I've gone back in time, before humanity, to a vision of the past where the monuments lurk over the valley like gods watching over a silent earth. I half expect a dinosaur to wander out from behind the red rocks.

"Was that your girlfriend back there?" I ask.

"Yes. We've been together 6 months and I'm hoping to make it much longer."

Our horses start as a pack of mustangs gallop out from behind a rock formation called The Totem Pole.

"There are wild horses all over the valley! We have caught and tamed many of them for our stables."

"That's incredible. Have you been riding horses all your life?"

"Since I was kid. I took 10 years off and lived in North Dakota, but I have family here so I came back."

The sun is almost all the way gone, and the valley gains somber hues of dark purple and orange. Spud neighs nervously and then bucks me off the saddle a foot or two.

"He probably just smells a bobcat," the horse tamer said nonchalantly. "They come out at night, and have great eyesight."

Slightly dispirited by this information, I give Spud another prod and whistle to pick up the pace. But then we round the corner of the Thunderbird Mesa and the whole valley opens up to the north, each monument painted with the varied palette of the sun's last rays. As if by some unspoken agreement, we both pull back on the reins and pause a moment, side by side. For some reason, it felt almost sacred.

"I've done this tour a hundred times, and it never gets old."

The Hitchhikers (Kayenta, Arizona)

Picking up a hitchhiker was one of the last things on my trip's bucket list. I had hitchhiked before so I felt I had a cosmic debt to repay. Little did I know that I'd be pulling over for not one, but two hitchhikers today.

"We're going in to town to buy coal," the husband said, closing the passenger seat door. "As you can see there's not much wood around here for fires."

I spotted the pair, an older Navajo couple, with their thumbs in the air on the side of Highway 163. It was just after sunrise about a mile south of Monument Valley.

"Glad I could give you a ride then," I say. "It got pretty cold last night! Were y'all gonna walk the 20 miles to Kayenta?"

"We've done it before," says the wife from the backseat. "But normally there is someone going that way who can take us. We usually only go into town once a month or so to attend a community meeting or buy supplies. Otherwise, we stay on our land and take care of the animals."

"What kind of animals do you have?"

"Mostly sheep," says the husband. "I used to work leading horseback rides around the valley, until I had an injury. Look, there's Dolly Parton!"

A bit taken aback at the non sequitur, I follow the man's pointed finger across the horizon to a large rock formation.

"It's actually called The Turtle," his wife says, shaking her head. "But that's what he calls it."

"You see it, don't you?" he says again, laughing.

The shadow across the mesa shifts as we whiz south on the highway, and now I understand the husband's unique view on the natural wonder.

"Right here is great!" says the woman, pointing at a small lodge on the side of the road. This must be the community center she mentioned. "We have a meeting this morning first before we get the coal."

The couple slowly emerge from the car and give a hesitant wave of thanks as they leave the highway. In a remote area such as this, relying on the kindness of strangers is really the only transportation option if you don't have money for a car. Without any fuss, they had just completed their customary, monthly hitchhiking commute into town.

SLOW

P.K. 3699
MIDWAY USA

148 AJR

1839 224
ILL 1950

BERNALILLO
66DINER
New Mexico USA
Land of Enchantment

HNR-748

273-598
MINNESOTA

PARKING FOR

WILDLIFE
MANAGEMENT
AREA
Operation
Game Thief
1-800-432-4213

20-118
NEW MEXICO

1889

66
DINER

Pepsi-Cola
ICE COLD

DANGER
KEEP OUT

QUALITY CHEKD.

ONLY

All Others Will Be
Pounded Into Flatware

1953
19 550

R 6720

68-604
NEW MEXICO

53 LAND OF ENCHANTMENT
25 192
NEW MEXICO

ROAD

The Aspiring Mechanic (Albuquerque, New Mexico)

Route 66 is an American a tradition right up there with baseball and apple pie. Known as "The Mother Road", this 1920s highway ran from Chicago, Illinois to Santa Monica, California. Diners, motels, and mom-and-pop shops sprang up along the road as Americans migrated west during the hard times of the 1930s. Unfortunately, Eisenhower's Interstate Highway System of the 1950s replaced almost the entirety of this historic route.

Today, for example, you'll probably be doing 75 next to long-haul truckers on I-40 if you're traveling east in New Mexico from Gallup to Albuquerque. However, if you keep an eye out, you'll see signs for "Historic Route 66" where you can pull off the interstate and slow it down to a cool 55 on a semi-deserted stretch of road. It's a welcome change of pace for the cross country traveler – the interstate teaches you to find speed at all costs and focus on getting to the destination, all while feeling trapped among convoys of 18 wheelers or rushed by a tailgating sports car. On Route 66, you can take a deep breath, roll the windows down, and take in the sights at your own pace.

When you hit Albuquerque, Route 66 turns into Central Ave. There you can find the 66 Diner, a 50s style spot with burgers, fries, and milkshakes.

"What's your favorite shake?" I ask the teenager manning the counter.

"Pumpkin pie is the special right now." He points to the board behind me head. "I don't drink them anymore though."

"Why not?"

"We get free shakes here."

Undaunted by the typical, terse teenager response, I press on.

"I would drink like 10 shakes a day if I worked here and they were free..." I say, laughing.

"You would at first. Then you'd stop. Most people working here lose their sweet tooth after 2 months."

"I guess that makes sense. Too much of a good thing. How much longer do you think you'll keeping working here?"

"I'm in a charter school because of behavior problems – I mostly just talk back to teachers a lot, in case you're wondering – but I'll work here on the side until I graduate in the spring. Then I'm going to become a mechanic, probably for Toyota. I spent all my money to buy a Lotus, and they have all Toyota parts. I put in a new engine for only $700."

"Impressive. I don't know anything about cars."

"Well that's why there are people like me. Here's your milkshake!"

What Chatting With America Taught Me

"If a man can keep alert and imaginative, an error is a possibility, a chance at something new; to him, wandering and wondering are part of the same process, and he is most mistaken, most in error, whenever he quits exploring."

I've been home from my journey for about a month now, and I've finally had a chance to reflect on my time chatting with America. This quote comes from a book called Blue Highways, written by a man named William Least Heat-Moon. This summer, as I walking along a quiet residential street in D.C., I saw it on the top of a stack of books in a cardboard box. Someone had scrawled, "Free – Please Take!" on the side of the box in Sharpie. In the book, the author describes his journey on the "blue highways" of America. On an old style Rand McNally road atlas, these were the smaller roads that connected off-the-beaten-path parts of the country (as opposed to the red highways that were more major thoroughfares).

"Keep alert and imaginative." That's the heart of it. If you can do that every day, you will find chatting opportunities galore. Keep your head up from your phone, and imagine what adventure might be just around an interesting corner. The problem is, it's tough work. Some days we'll be able to do it, and some days we won't be able to lift our eyes from our own shoelaces of self-centeredness. For every moment where I got to truly connect with someone and chat, there was a moment where I chose not to engage and may have missed more beautiful stories.

I started the trip with the goal of getting to know people without having any specific agenda. I didn't take their picture, I didn't have any set interview questions. Just conversation. Here a few things I learned:

1. People are willing to open up about really deep and powerful things in their life if you just ask a few well-crafted questions and show them that you really want to hear their story.
2. Everyone has interesting things to tell you about themselves if you do the work to uncover them.
3. You can encounter extraordinary experiences just by keeping your eyes and ears open during your everyday life.

Thank you to all the friendly folks along my trip. Some of you I may see again, and some of you I may not. To all the beautiful parts of the country I didn't get to see and all the good people I didn't get to chat with, I hope to see you one day. To everyone reading this, may you find great joy and comfort in pursuing conversation for its own sake.

Keep alert and imaginative. Happy chatting!

www.ingramcontent.com/pod-product-compliance
Lightning Source LLC
Chambersburg PA
CBHW040711150426

42811CB00061B/1816